Frequently Asked Interview Q & A in Sca.

Scala Programming

By Bandana Ojha

Introduction

The authors of this book " Frequently asked Interview Q & A in Scala" have conducted so many Java/J2EE/Scala interviews at various companies and meticulously collected the most effective scala interview notes with simple, straightforward explanations. Rather than going through comprehensive, textbook-sized reference guides, this book includes only the information required immediately for scala interview to start their career in Information technology. Answers of all the questions are short and to the point. This book contains 100+ questions and answers and we assure that you will get 90% frequently asked Scala interview questions going through this book. It will clear your fundamentals, concepts and boost your confidence to appear any Scala interview in any companies anywhere in the world whether it is telephonic or face to face.

Wishing good luck to all my readers!!!

1) What is Scala?

Scala is a general-purpose programming language providing support for both functional and Object-Oriented programming.

2. What is tail-recursion in Scala?

There are several situations where programmers have to write functions that are recursive in nature. The main problem with recursive functions is that, it may eat up all the allocated stack space. To overcome this situation, Scala compiler provides a mechanism "tail recursion" to optimize these recursive functions so that it does not create new stack space, instead uses the current function stack space. To qualify for this, annotation "@annotation.tailrec" has to be used before defining the function and recursive call has to be the last statement, then only the function will compile otherwise, it will give an error.

3. What are 'traits' in Scala?

'Traits' are used to define object types specified by the signature of the supported methods. Scala allows to be partially implemented but traits may not have constructor parameters. A trait consists of method and field definition, by mixing them into classes it can be reused.

4. Who is the father of Scala programming language?

Martin Oderskey, a German computer scientist, is the father of Scala programming language.

5. What are case classes in Scala?

Case classes are standard classes declared with a special modifier case. Case classes export their constructor parameters and provide a recursive decomposition mechanism through pattern matching. The constructor parameters of case classes are treated as public values and can be accessed directly. For a case class, companion objects and its associated method also get generated automatically. All the methods in the class, as well, methods in the companion objects are generated based on the parameter list. The only advantage of Case class is that it automatically generates the methods from the parameter list.

6. What is the super class of all classes in Scala?

In Java, the super class of all classes (Java API Classes or User Defined Classes) is java.lang.Object. In the same way in Scala, the super class of all classes or traits is "Any" class.

Any class is defined in scala package like "scala.Any".

7. What is a 'Scala Set'? What are methods through which operation sets are expressed?

Scala set is a collection of pairwise elements of the same type. Scala set does not contain any duplicate elements. There are two kinds of sets, mutable and immutable.

8. What is a Scala Map?

Scala Map is a collection of key value pairs wherein the value in a map can be retrieved using the key. Values in a Scala Map are not unique, but the keys are unique. Scala supports two kinds of maps- mutable and immutable. By default, Scala supports immutable map and to make use of the mutable map, programmers must import the scala.collection.mutable.Map class explicitly. When programmers want to use mutable and immutable map together in the same program then the mutable map can be accessed as mutable.map and the immutable map can just be accessed with the name of the map.

9. Name two significant differences between a trait and an abstract class.

Abstract classes have constructors with zero or more parameters while traits do not; a class can extend any number of traits but only one abstract class.

10. What is the use of tuples in Scala?

Scala tuples combine a fixed number of items together so that they can be passed around as whole. A tuple is immutable and can hold objects with different types, unlike an array or list.

11. What do you understand by a closure in Scala?

A closure is also known as an anonymous function whose return value depends upon the value of the variables declared outside the function.

12. What do you understand by Implicit Parameter?

Wherever, we require that function could be invoked without passing all the parameters, we use implicit parameter. We provide the default values for all the parameters or parameters which we want to be used as implicit. When the function is invoked without passing the implicit parameters, local value of that parameter is used. We need to use implicit keyword to make a value, function parameter or variable as implicit.

13. What is the companion object in Scala?

A companion object is an object with the same name as a class or trait and is defined in the same source file as the associated file or trait. A companion object differs from other objects as it has access rights to the class/trait that other objects do not. In particular it can access methods and fields that are private in the class/trait.

14. What are the advantages of Scala Language?

Advantages of Scala Language:-

- Simple and Concise Code

- Very Expressive Code

- More Readable Code

- 100% Type-Safe Language

- Immutability and No Side-Effects

- More Reusable Code

- More Modularity

- Do More with Less Code

- Supports all OOP Features

- Supports all FP Features. Highly Functional.

- Less Error Prone Code

- Better Parallel and Concurrency Programming

- Highly Scalable and Maintainable code

- Highly Productivity

- Distributed Applications

- Full Java Interoperability

- Powerful Scala DSLs available

15. What are the major drawbacks of Scala Language?

Drawbacks of Scala Language:-

-       Less Readable Code

-       Bit tough to Understand the Code for beginners

-       Complex Syntax to learn

-       Less Backward Compatibility

16. What is Akka, Play, and Sleek in Scala?

Akka is a concurrency framework in Scala which uses Actor based model for building highly concurrent, distributed, and resilient message-driven applications on the JVM. It uses high-level abstractions like Actor, Future, and Stream to simplify coding for concurrent applications. It also provides load balancing, routing, partitioning, and adaptive cluster management. If you are interested in learning Akka,

17. What is 'Unit' and '()' in Scala?

The 'Unit' is a type like void in Java. You can say it is a Scala equivalent of the void in Java, while still providing the language with an abstraction over the Java platform. The empty tuple '()' is a term representing a Unit value in Scala.

18. What is the difference between a normal class and a case class in Scala?

Following are some key differences between a case class and a normal class in Scala:

- case class allows pattern matching on it.

- you can create instances of case class without using the new keyword

- equals(), hashcode() and toString() method are automatically generated for case classes in Scala

- Scala automatically generate accessor methods for all constructor argument

19. What are High Order Functions in Scala?

High order functions are functions that can receive or return other functions. Common examples in Scala are the filter, map, and flatMap functions, which receive other functions as arguments.

20. Which Scala library is used for functional programming?

Scalaz library has purely functional data structures that complement the standard Scala library. It has pre-defined set of foundational type classes like Monad, Functor, etc.

21. What is the best scala style checker tool available for play and scala based applications?

Scalastyle is best Scala style checker tool available for Play and Scala based applications.

Scalastyle observes the Scala source code and indicates potential problems with it. It has three separate plug-ins to supports the following build tools:

SBT

Maven

Gradle

22. What is the difference between concurrency and parallelism?

When several computations execute sequentially during overlapping time periods it is referred to as concurrency whereas when processes are executed simultaneously it is known as parallelism. Parallel collection, Futures and Async library are examples of achieving parallelism in Scala.

23. What is the difference between a Java method and a Scala function?

Scala function can be treated as a value. It can be assigned to a val or var, or even returned from another function, which is not possible in Java. Though Java 8 brings lambda expression which also makes function as a first-class object, which means you can pass a function to a method just like you pass an object as an argument. See here to learn more about the difference between Scala and Java.

24. What is the difference between Function and Method in Scala?

Scala supports both functions and methods. We use same syntax to define functions and methods, there is no syntax difference.

However, they have one minor difference:

We can define a method in a Scala class or trait. Method is associated with an object (An instance of a Class). We can call a method by using an instance of a Class. We cannot use a Scala Method directly without using object.

Function is not associated with a class or trait. It is defined in a Scala Package. We can access functions without using objects, like Java's Static Methods.

25. What is Extractor in Scala?

In Scala, Extractor is used to decompose or disassemble an object into its parameters (or components).

26. Is Scala a Pure OOP Language?

Yes, Scala is a Pure Object-Oriented Programming Language because in Scala, everything is an Object, and everything is a value. Functions are values and values are Objects.

Scala does not have primitive data types and does not have static members.

27. Is Java a pure OOP Language?

Java is not a Pure Object-Oriented Programming (OOP) Language because it supports the following two Non-OOP concepts:

Java supports primitive data types. They are not objects.

Java supports Static members. They are not related to objects.

28. Does Scala support Operator Overloading?

Scala supports Operator Overloading.

Scala has given this flexibility to Developer to decide which methods/functions name should use.

When we call 4 + 5 that means '+' is not an operator, it is a method available in Int class (or it's implicit type). Internally, this call is converted into "4.+(5)".

29. Does Java support Operator Overloading?

Java does not support Operator Overloading.

30. What are the default imports in Scala Language?

We know, java.lang is the default package imported into all Java Programs by JVM automatically. We don't need to import this package explicitly.

In the same way, the following are the default imports available in all Scala Programs:

java.lang package

Scala package

scala.PreDef

31. What is an Expression?

Expression is a value that means it will evaluate to a Value. As an Expression returns a value, we can assign it to a variable.

Example:- Scala's If condition, Java's Ternary operator.

32.What is a Statement? Difference between Expression and Statement?

Statement defines one or more actions or operations. That means Statement performs actions. As it does not return a value, we cannot assign it to a Variable.

Example:- Java's If condition.

33.What is the difference between Java's "If...Else" and Scala's "If..Else"?

Java's "If..Else":

In Java, "If..Else" is a statement, not an expression. It does not return a value and cannot assign it to a variable.

Example:-

```
int year;
if( count == 0)
   year = 2018;
else
   year = 2017;
```

Scala's "If..Else":

In Scala, "If..Else" is an expression. It evaluates a value i.e. returns a value. We can assign it to a variable.

```
val year = if( count == 0) 2018 else 2017
```

NOTE:-Scala's "If..Else" works like Java's Ternary Operator. We can use Scala's "If..Else" like Java's "If..Else" statement as shown below:

```
val year = 0
if( count == 0)
  year = 2018
else
  year = 2017
```

34. How to compile and run a Scala program?

You can use Scala compiler scalac to compile Scala program (like javac) and scala command to run them (like scala)

35.How to tell Scala to look into a class file for some Java class?

We can use -classpath argument to include a JAR in Scala's classpath, as shown below

```
$ scala -classpath jar
```

Alternatively, you can also use CLASSPATH environment variable.

36. What is the difference between a call-by-value and call-by-name parameter?

The main difference between a call-by-value and a call-by-name parameter is that the former is computed before calling the function, and the latter is evaluated when accessed.

37. What exactly is wrong with a recursive function that is not tail-recursive?

Answer: You run the risk of running out of stack space and thus throwing an exception.

38. What is the difference between var and value?

In scala, you can define a variable using either a, val or var keywords. The difference between val and var is, var is much like java declaration, but val is little different. We cannot change the reference to point to another reference, once the variable is declared using val. The variable defined using var keywords are mutable and can be changed any number of times.

39. What is scala anonymous function?

In a source code, anonymous functions are called 'function literals' and at run time, function literals are instantiated into objects called function values. Scala provides a relatively easy syntax for defining anonymous functions.

40. What is function currying in scala?

Currying is the technique of transforming a function that takes multiple arguments into a function that takes a single argument Many of the same techniques as language like Haskell and LISP are supported by Scala. Function currying is one of the least used and misunderstood one.

41. What do you understand by "Unit" and "()" in Scala?

Unit is a subtype of scala.anyval and is nothing but Scala equivalent of Java void that provides the Scala with an abstraction of the java platform. Empty tuple i.e. () in Scala is a term that represents unit value.

42. What's the difference 'Nil', 'Null', 'None' and 'Nothing' in Scala?

Null – It's a sub-type of AnyRef type in Scala Types hierarchy. As Scala runs on JVM, it uses NULL to provide the compatibility with Java null keyword, or in Scala terms, to provide type for null keyword, Null type exists. It represents the absence of type information for complex types that are inherited from AnyRef.

Nothing – It's a sub-type of all the types exists in Scala Types hierarchy. It helps in providing the return type for the operations that can affect a normal program's flow. It can only be used as a type, as instantiation of nothing cannot be done. It incorporates all types under AnyRef and AnyVal. Nothing is usually used as a return type for methods that have abnormal termination and result in an exception.

Nil – It's a handy way of initializing an empty list since, Nil, is an object, which extends List [Nothing].

None – In programming, there are many circumstances, where we unexpectedly received null for the methods we call. In java these are handled using try/catch or left unattended causing errors in the program. Scala provides a very graceful way of handling those situations. In cases, where you don't know, if you would be able to return a value as expected, we can use Option [T]. It is an abstract class, with just two sub-classes, Some [T] and none. With this, we can tell users that, the method might return a T of type Some [T] or it might return none.

43. What is Lazy Evaluation?

Lazy Evaluation means evaluating program at run-time on-demand that means when clients access the program then only its evaluated.

The difference between "val" and "lazy val" is that "val" is used to define variables which are evaluated eagerly and "lazy val" is also used to define variables but they are evaluated lazily.

44. What is call-by-name?

Call-by-name means evaluates method/function parameters only when we need them, or we access them. If we don't use them, then it does not evaluate them.

45. Does Scala and Java support call-by-name?

Scala supports both call-by-value and call-by-name function parameters. However, Java supports only call-by-value, but not call-by-name.

46. What is the difference between call-by-value and call-by-name function parameters?

Difference between call-by-value and call-by-name:

The major difference between these two are described below:

In Call-by-name, the function parameters are evaluated only whenever they are needed but not when the function is called.

In Call-by-value, the function parameters are evaluated when the function is called.

In Call-by-value, the parameters are evaluated before executing function and they are evaluated only once irrespective of how many times we used them in that function.

In Call-by-name, the parameters are evaluated whenever we access them, and they are evaluated each time we use them in that function.

47. What do you understand by apply and unapply methods in Scala?

apply and unapply methods in Scala are used for mapping and unmapping data between form and model data.

Apply method – Used to assemble an object from its components. For example, if we want to create an Employee object then use the two components firstName and lastName and compose the Employee object using the apply method.

Unapply method – Used to decompose an object from its components. It follows the reverse process of apply method. So, if you have an employee object, it can be decomposed into two components- firstName and lastName.

48. What is an anonymous function in Scala?

Anonymous Function is also a Function, but it does not have any function name. It is also known as a Function Literal.

49.What are the advantages of Anonymous Function/Function Literal in Scala?

The advantages of Anonymous Function/Function Literal in Scala:

We can assign a Function Literal to variable

We can pass a Function Literal to another function/method

We can return a Function Literal as another function/method result/return value

50. What is the difference between unapply and apply, when would you use them?

Unapply is a method that needs to be implemented by an object in order for it to be an extractor. Extractors are used in pattern matching to access an object constructor parameter. It's the opposite of a constructor.

The apply method is a special method that allows you to write someObject(params) instead of someObject.apply(params). This usage is common in case classes, which contain a companion object with the apply method that allows the nice syntax to instantiate a new object without the new keyword.

51. What is the difference between a trait and an abstract class in Scala?

Here are some key differences between a trait and an abstract class in Scala:

A class can inherit from multiple traits but only one abstract class.

Abstract classes can have constructor parameters as well as type parameters. Traits can have only type parameters. For example, you can't say trait t(i: Int) {}; the iparameter is illegal.

Abstract classes are fully interoperable with Java. You can call them from Java code without any wrappers. On the other hand, Traits are fully interoperable only if they do not contain any implementation code. See here to learn more about Abstract class in Java and OOP.

52. Can a companion object in Scala access the private members of its companion class in Scala?

According to the private access specifier, private members can be accessed only within that class, but Scala's companion object and class provide special access to private members. A companion object can access all the private members of a companion class. Similarly, a companion class can access all the private members of companion objects.

53. What are scala variables?

Values and variables are two shapes that come in Scala. A value variable is constant and cannot be changed once assigned. It is immutable, while a regular variable, on the other hand, is mutable, and you can change the value.

The two types of variables are

var myVar : Int=0;

val myVal: Int=1;

54. Mention the difference between an object and a class ?

A class is a definition for a description. It defines a type in terms of methods and composition of other types. A class is a blueprint of the object. While, an object is a singleton, an instance of a class which is unique. An anonymous class is created for every object in the code, it inherits from whatever classes you declared object to implement.

55. What is the difference between val and var in Scala?

The val keyword stands for value and var stands for variable. You can use keyword val to store values, these are immutable, and cannot change once assigned. On the other hand, keyword var is used to create variables, which are values that can change after being set. If you try to modify a val, the compiler will throw an error. It is like the final variable in Java or const in C++.

56. What is the difference between Array and List in Scala?

Arrays are always Mutable whereas List is always Immutable.

Once created, we can change Array values where as we cannot change List Object.

Arrays are fixed-size data structures whereas List is variable-sized data structures. List's size is automatically increased or decreased based on its operations we perform on it.

Arrays are Invariants whereas Lists are Covariant.

57. What is "Type Inference" in Scala?

Types can be inferred by the Scala Compiler at compile-time. It is known as "Type Inference". Types means Data type or Result type. We use Types at many places in Scala programs like Variable types, Object types, Method/Function Parameter types, Method/Function return types etc.

In simple words, determining the type of a variable or expression or object etc. at compile-time by compiler is known as "Type Inference".

58. What is Eager Evaluation?

Eager Evaluation means evaluating program at compile-time or program deployment-time irrespective of clients are using that program or not.

59. What is guard in Scala's 'for-Comprehension' construct?

In Scala, for-comprehension construct has an if clause which is used to write a condition to filter some elements and generate new collection. This if clause is also known as "Guard".

If that guard is true, then add that element to new collection. Otherwise, it does not add that element to original collection.

60. Why scala prefers immutability?

Scala prefers immutability in design and in many cases uses it as default. Immutability can help when dealing with equality issues or concurrent programs.

61. What are the considerations you need to have when using Scala streams?

Streams in Scala are a type of lazy collection, which are created using starting element and then recursively generated using those elements. Streams are like a List, except that, elements are added only when they are accessed, hence "lazy". Since streams are lazy in terms of adding elements, they can be unbounded also, and once the elements are added, they are cached. Since Streams can be unbounded, and all the values are computed at the time of access, programmers need to be careful on using methods which are not transformers, as it may result in java.lang.OutOfMemoryErrors.

stream.max

stream.size

stream.sum

62. Differentiate between Array and List in Scala.

List is an immutable recursive data structure whilst array is a sequential mutable data structure.

Lists are covariant whilst array are invariants.

The size of a list automatically increases or decreases based on the operations that are performed on it i.e. a list in Scala is a variable-sized data structure whilst an array is fixed size data structure.

63. Which keyword is used to define a function in Scala?

A function is defined in Scala using the def keyword. This may sound familiar to Python developers as Python also uses def to define a function.

64. What is Monad in Scala?

A monad is an object that wraps another object in Scala. It helps to perform the data manipulation of the underlying object, instead of manipulating the object directly.

65. Is Scala statically-typed language?

Yes, Scala is a statically-typed language.

66.What is Statically-Typed Language and What is Dynamically-Typed Language?

Statically-Typed Language means that Type checking is done at compile-time by compiler, not at run-time. Dynamically-Typed Language means that Type checking is done at run-time, not at compile-time by compiler.

67. What is the difference between unapply and apply, when would you use them?

unapply is a method that needs to be implemented by an object in order for it to be an extractor. Extractors are used in pattern matching to access an object constructor parameter. It's the opposite of a constructor.

The apply method is a special method that allows you to write someObject(params) instead of someObject.apply(params). This usage is common in case classes, which contain a companion object with the apply method that allows the nice syntax to instantiate a new object without the new keyword.

68. What is Unit in Scala?

In Scala, Unit is used to represent "No value" or "No Useful value". Unit is a final class defined in "scala" package that is "scala.Unit".

69. What is the difference between Java's void and Scala's Unit?

Unit is something like Java's void. But they have few differences.

Java's void does not any value. It is nothing.

Scala's Unit has one value ()

() is the one and only value of type Unit in Scala. However, there are no values of type void in Java.

Java's void is a keyword. Scala's Unit is a final class.

Both are used to represent a method or function is not returning anything.

70. What is "App" in Scala?

In Scala, App is a trait defined in scala package like "scala.App". It defines main method. If an Object or a Class extends this trait, then they will become as Scala Executable programs automatically because they will inherit main method from Application.

71. What is the use of Scala's App?

The main advantage of using App is that we don't need to write main method. The main drawback of using App is that we should use same name "args" to refer command line argument because scala.App's main() method uses this name.

71. What are option, some and none in scala?

'Option' is a Scala generic type that can either be 'some' generic value or none. 'Queue' often uses it to represent primitives that may be null.

73. What is Scala Future?

Scala Future is a monadic collection, which starts a background task. It is an object which holds the potential value or future value, which would be available after the task is completed. It also provides various operations to further chain the operations or to extract the value. Future also provide various call-back functions like onComplete, OnFailure, onSuccess to name a few, which makes Future a complete concurrent task class.

74. How it differs from java's Future class?

The main and foremost difference between Scala's Future and Java's Future class is that the later does not provide promises/callbacks operations. The only way to retrieve the result is Future.get () in Java.

75. What do you understand by diamond problem and how does Scala resolve this?

Multiple inheritance problem is referred to as the Deadly diamond problem or diamond problem. The inability to decide on which implementation of the method to choose is referred to as the Diamond Problem in Scala. Suppose say classes B and C both inherit from class A, while class D inherits from both class B and C. Now while implementing multiple inheritance if B and C override some method from class A, there is a confusion and dilemma always on which implementation D should inherit. This is what is referred to as diamond problem. Scala resolves diamond problem through the concept of Traits and class linearization rules.

76. What is the difference between == in Java and Scala?

Scala has more intuitive notion of equality. The == operator will automatically run the instance's equals method, rather than doing Java style comparison to check that two objects are the same reference. By the way, you can still check for referential equality by using eq method. In short, Java == operator compare references while Scala calls the equals() method. You can also read the difference between == and equals() in Java to learn more about how they behave in Java.

77. What is REPL in Scala? What is the use of Scala's REPL?

REPL stands for Read-Evaluate Print Loop. We can pronounce it as 'ripple'. In Scala, REPL is acts as an Interpreter to execute Scala code from command prompt. That's why REPL is also known as Scala CLI(Command Line Interface) or Scala command-line shell.

The main purpose of REPL is that to develop and test small snippets of Scala code for practice purpose. It is very useful for Scala Beginners to practice basic programs.

78. What are the similarities between Scala's Int and Java's java.lang.Integer?

Similarities between Scala's Int and Java's java.lang.Integer are

Both are classes.

Both are used to represent integer numbers.

Both are 32-bit signed integers.

79.What are the differences between Scala's Int and Java's java.lang.Integer?

Differences between Scala's Int and Java's java.lang.Integer are

Scala's Int class does not implement Comparable interface.

Java's java.lang.Integer class implements Comparable interface.

80. What is the relationship between Int and RichInt in Scala?

Java's Integer is something like Scala's Int and RichInt. RichInt is a final class defined in scala.runtime package like "scala.runtime.RichInt".

In Scala, the Relationship between Int and RichInt is that when we use Int in a Scala program, it will automatically convert into RichInt to utilize all methods available in that Class. We can say that RichInt is an Implicit class of Int.

81. What is the best framework to generate rest api documentation for scala-based applications?

Swagger is the best tool for this purpose. It is very simple and open-source tool for generating REST APIs documentation with JSON for Scala-based applications.

If you use Play with Scala to develop your REST API, then use play-swagger module for REST API documentation.

If you use Spray with Scala to develop your REST API, then use spray-swagger module for REST API documentation.

82. What is the use of Auxiliary Constructors in Scala?

Auxiliary Constructor is the secondary constructor in Scala declared using the keywords "this" and "def". The main purpose of using auxiliary constructors is to overload constructors. Just like in Java, we can provide implementation for different kinds of constructors so that the right one is invoked based on the requirements. Every auxiliary constructor in Scala should differ in the number of parameters or in data types.

83. How does yield work in Scala?

The yield keyword if specified before the expression, the value returned from every expression, will be returned as the collection. The yield keyword is very useful, when there is a need, you want to use the return value of expression. The collection returned can be used the normal collection and iterate over in another loop.

84. What are the different types of Scala identifiers?

There four types of Scala identifiers

Alpha numeric identifiers

Operator identifiers

Mixed identifiers

Literal identifiers

85. What are the different types of Scala literals?

The different types of literals in scala are

Integer literals

Floating point literals

Boolean literals

Symbol literals

Character literals

String literals

Multi-Line strings

86. What is SBT? What is the best build tool to develop play and scala applications?

SBT stands for Scala Build Tool. Its a Simple Build Tool to develop Scala-based applications.

Most of the people uses SBT Build tool for Play and Scala Applications. For example, IntelliJ IDEA Scala Plugin by default uses SBT as Build tool for this purpose.

87. What is the difference between :: and ::: in Scala?

:: and ::: are methods available in List class.

:: method is used to append an element to the beginning of the list.

And ::: method is used to concatenate the elements of a given list in front of this list.

:: method works as a cons operator for List class. Here 'cons' stands for construct.

::: method works as a concatenation operator for List class.

88.What is the difference between #:: and #::: in Scala?

#:: and #::: are methods available in Stream class

#:: method words as a cons operator for Stream class. Here 'cons' stands for construct.

#:: method is used to append a given element at beginning of the stream.

#::: method is used to concatenate a given stream at beginning of the stream.

89. What is the use of '???' in Scala-based Applications?

This '???' three question marks is not an operator, a method in Scala. It is used to mark a method which is 'In Progress' that means Developer should provide implementation for that one.

90. What is the best Scala style checker tool available for Play and Scala based applications?

Scalastyle is best Scala style checker tool available for Play and Scala based applications.

Scalastyle observes our Scala source code and indicates potential problems with it. It has three separate plug-ins to supports the following build tools:

SBT

Maven

Gradle

It has two separate plug-ins to supports the following two IDEs:

IntelliJ IDEA

Eclipse IDE

91. How Scala supports both Highly Scalable and Highly Performance applications?

As Scala supports Multi-Paradigm Programming(Both OOP and FP) and uses Actor Concurrency Model, we can develop very highly Scalable and high-performance applications very easily.

92.What are the available Build Tools to develop Play and Scala based Applications?

The following three are most popular available Build Tools to develop Play and Scala Applications:

SBT

Maven

Gradle

93. What is Either in Scala?

In Scala, either is an abstract class. It is used to represent one value of two possible types. It takes two type parameters: Either[A,B].

94. What are Left and Right in Scala? Explain Either/Left/Right Design Pattern in Scala?

It exactly has two subtypes: Left and Right. If Either[A,B] represents an instance A that means it is Left. If it represents an instance B that means it is Right.

This is known as Either/Left/Right Design Pattern in Scala.

95. How many public class files are possible to define in Scala source file?

In Java, we can define at-most one public class/interface in a Source file. Unlike Java, Scala supports multiple public classes in the same source file.

We can define any number of public classes/interfaces/traits in a Scala Source file.

96. What is Nothing in Scala?

In Scala, nothing is a Type (final class). It is defined at the bottom of the Scala Type System that means it is a subtype of anything in Scala. There are no instances of Nothing.

97.What's the difference between the following terms and types in Scala: 'Nil', 'Null', 'None', and 'Nothing' in Scala?

Even though they look similar, there are some subtle differences between them, let's see them one by one:

Nil represents the end of a List.

Null denotes the absence of value but in Scala, more precisely, Null is a type that represents the absence of type information for complex types that are inherited from AnyRef. It is different than null in Java.

None is the value of an Option if it has no value in it.

Nothing is the bottom type of the entire Scala type system, incorporating all types under AnyVal and AnyRef. Nothing is commonly used as a return type from a method that does not terminate normally and throws an exception

98. How to you create Singleton classes in Scala?

Scala introduces a new object keyword, which is used to represent Singleton classes. These are the class with just one instance and their method can be thought of as like Java's static methods. Here is a Singleton class in Scala:

package test

object Singleton{

  def sum(l: List[Int]): Int = l.sum

}

This sum method is available globally, and can be referred to, or imported, as the test.Singleton.sum. A singleton object in Scala can also extend classes and traits.

99. What is 'Option' and how is it used in Scala?

The 'Option' in Scala is like Optional of Java 8. It is a wrapper type that avoids the occurrence of a NullPointerException in your code by giving you default value in case object is null. When you call get() from

Option it can return a default value if the value is null. More importantly, Option provides the ability to differentiate within the type system those values that can be nulled and those that cannot be nulled.

100. What is the difference between a call-by-value and call-by-name parameter?

The main difference between a call-by-value and a call-by-name parameter is that the former is computed before calling the function, and the later is evaluated when accessed.

101. What is default access modifier in Scala? Does Scala have "public" keyword?

In Scala, if we don't mention any access modifier to a method, function, trait, object or class, the default access modifier is "public". Even for Fields also, "public" is the default access modifier.

Because of this default feature, Scala does not have "public" keyword.

102. Is Scala an Expression-Based Language or Statement-Based Language?

In Scala, everything is a value. All Expressions or Statements evaluates to a Value. We can assign Expression, Function, Closure, Object etc. to a Variable. So, Scala is an Expression-Oriented Language.

103. Is Java an Expression-Based Language or Statement-Based Language?

In Java, Statements are not Expressions or Values. We cannot assign them to a Variable. So, Java is not an Expression-Oriented Language. It is a Statement-Based Language.

104. Mention Some keywords which are used by Java and not required in Scala?

Java uses the following keywords extensively:

'public' keyword – to define classes, interfaces, variables etc.

'static' keyword – to define static members.

105.Why Scala does not require them?

Scala does not require these two keywords. Scala does not have 'public' and 'static' keywords.

In Scala, default access modifier is 'public' for classes, traits, methods/functions, fields etc. That's why, 'public' keyword is not required.

To support OOP principles, Scala team has avoided 'static' keyword. That's why Scala is a Pure-OOP Language. It is very tough to deal static members in Concurrency applications.

Please check this out:

Our other best-selling books

500+ Java & J2EE Interview Questions & Answers-Java & J2EE
Programming

200+ Frequently Asked Interview Questions & Answers in iOS
Development

200 + Frequently Asked Interview Q & A in SQL , PL/SQL,
Database Development & Administration

100+ Frequently Asked Interview Questions & Answers in Scala

100+ Frequently Asked Interview Q & A in Swift Programming

100+ Frequently Asked Interview Q & A in Python Programming

100+ Frequently Asked Interview Questions & Answers in
Android Development

100+ most Frequently Asked Interview Questions & Answers in
Manual Testing

Frequently asked Interview Q & A in Java programming

Frequently Asked Interview Questions & Answers in J2EE

Frequently asked Interview Q & A in Mobile Testing

Frequently asked Interview Q & A in Test Automation-Selenium
Testing

****

Please check out our other bestselling books

www.ingramcontent.com/pod-product-compliance
Lightning Source LLC
LaVergne TN
LVHW042307060326
832902LV00009B/1316